BARRINGTON
ON SQUASH

BARRINGTON ON SQUASH

JONAH BARRINGTON

STANLEY PAUL / LONDON

Stanley Paul & Co Ltd
3 Fitzroy Square, London W1

An imprint of the Hutchinson Group

London Melbourne Sydney Auckland
Wellington Johannesburg Cape Town
and agencies throughout the world

First published 1973
Second impression May 1974
Third impression June 1975
© Jonah Barrington 1973

Printed in Great Britain by litho by The Anchor Press Ltd
and bound by Wm Brendon & Son Ltd
both of Tiptree, Essex

ISBN 0 09 115770 6

ACKNOWLEDGEMENT

There was a time before beginning work on this book when the artist, Duncan Mil, generally knew nothing of the art of Squash. The speed with which he mastered the many problems of portrayal was in itself remarkable. I would like to thank him for bestowing his talent so vividly through-out the book.

CONTENTS

INTRODUCTION

The completion at last of this book has been considered by my publishers almost as much a triumph as the winning of an Open Title! My industry is still much confined to preparation for competitive match play and there have been many worthy souls who have shown remarkable stamina in the extraction from me of the text.

However on the happy occasion of final proofing I am again provided with a rich vein of memories, so many parts of an extremely satisfying whole.

The basic lessons are a strong link with my own teachers, the fabulous Khans, and I treasure the countless happy moments I have spent with my mentor, Nasrullah. His influence on me is expressed throughout these pages and my debt to both Naz and his cousin Azam is clearly shown. No wonder 1966 was a marvellous year for me, fashioned as I was by two men, one the finest coach and the other the supreme player of the day.

The matches, which I have recounted, in the main with the help of Rex Bellamy and Dicky Rutnagur, were traumatic at the time and still quickened the pulse as they were recalled here.

Strangely perhaps, it is in the sphere of training that I have been given the fullest satisfaction. The lethargy of my youth has since bred in me the most earnest desire to explore my physical potential. Those punishing games with Azam at the New Grampians Club, the searing sessions at the Mayfair Gymnasium, and the pain-filled hours spent running to exhaustion, have all generated in me a necessary self-respect and confidence in the partial mastery of my body and, perhaps more important, my mind. The sheer stimulation and marvellous sense of well-being which springs from physical fitness have continued to make the effort immensely worthwhile.

I am often asked what is my strongest memory in the sport, and many people are surprised when I reply that I treasure a training session I once did with Ron Clarke, the greatest distance athlete of his day. First, we did some court training and he was excellent at that. Then we ran, but not for long, as even a strained groin could not prevent him from searching me out after a brief burst!

LESSON 1
THE GRIP

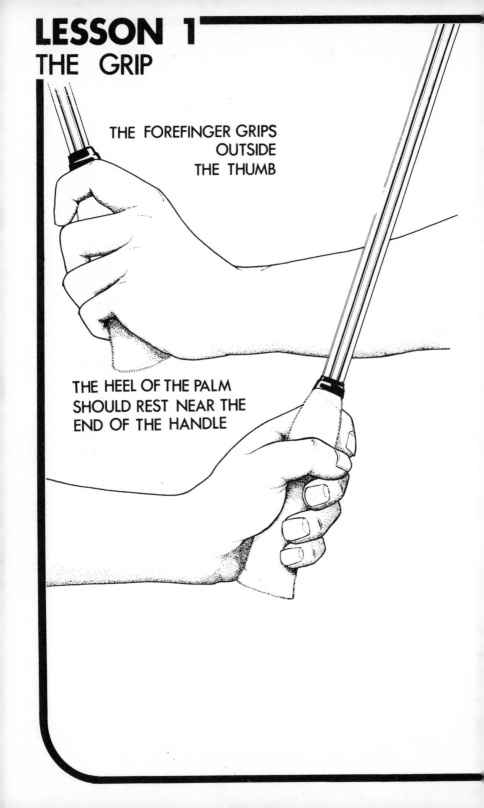

THE FOREFINGER GRIPS
OUTSIDE
THE THUMB

THE HEEL OF THE PALM
SHOULD REST NEAR THE
END OF THE HANDLE

I am left-handed; you just could be right-handed.

There has to be a beginning to everything and in Squash the beginner will face the moment when he or she will hold a racket for the first time. All that follows in this manual will be the better for a correct grip, and too frequently one see players at all levels making simple mistakes because the initial instruction was just not available or unhappily was even wrong.

The most important thing for a beginner is to grip the racket properly for only then can he or she make sure progress in the striking of the ball. It is essential that the forefinger grips the handle of the racket outside the thumb and that it is not restricted inside the thumb with the other fingers—a very common fault.

The heel of the palm should rest near the end of the handle. When holding the racket upright, directly in front, a V should run between thumb and forefingers slightly to the right of the centre of the shaft. This grip allows for much more power plus control and allows for maximum relaxation of the forearm muscles, without the cramping effect of a less efficient grip.

If you want to remind yourself of the correct grip, then place the racket in front of you with the head pointing away as in the drawing and shake hands with it! Incidentally, the great Hashim Khan provided the ultimate exception to the rule—there will always be one or two. He held the racket well down the shaft throughout his days as the World Champion. However, as Hashim has grown older so has his stomach grown larger, and he now uses the orthodox grip which allows him to stretch less for the ball!!

LESSON 2
FOREHAND DRIVE

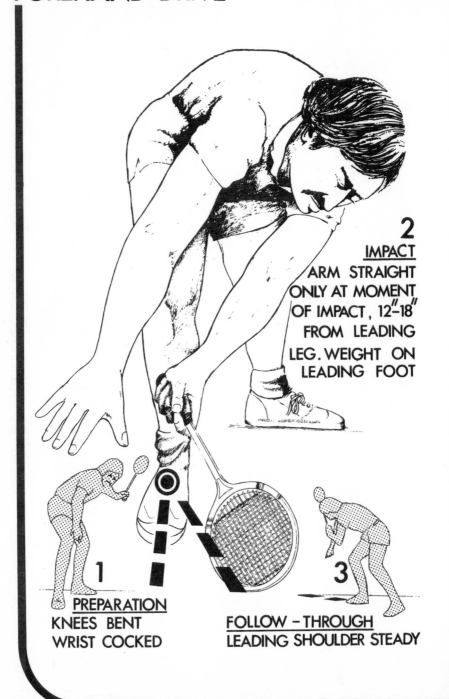

2
IMPACT
ARM STRAIGHT
ONLY AT MOMENT
OF IMPACT, 12"–18"
FROM LEADING
LEG. WEIGHT ON
LEADING FOOT

1
PREPARATION
KNEES BENT
WRIST COCKED

3
FOLLOW – THROUGH
LEADING SHOULDER STEADY

Once the pupil has been given the correct grip, he will quickly want to hit the ball. Tuition must still continue, otherwise the new enthusiast may well join that too large band of simpletons who feel that a man *must* be good if he can hit the ball really hard.

The average beginner has difficulty in timing his stroke and the only way he can achieve power is by developing a swing which would do justice to an executioner, but otherwise bears no relation to fair play.

A good style is pleasing to the eye and may well be developed, but a safe one is most necessary. Remember too that the most important factor is *where* the ball is finally despatched, not necessarily *how* it was despatched.

The forehand drive may be dealt with in three parts: preparation, impact, follow-through. These are all clearly seen in the drawings.

The swing is quite restricted in its action and the racket comes through quite close to the body with a firing action very similar to that of throwing a cricket ball at speed to a wicket-keeper.

The weight should initially be on the back foot with the wrist cocked, thereby keeping the racket head up.

The arm is bent and does not straighten until the moment of impact, which is ideally between 12 and 18 inches away from and just to the front of the leading leg. The weight will now be on that foot. The wrist does not break through but maintains its cocked position while the racket strikes the ball almost flat.

The follow-through should be full but should continue no further than the line of the body. Any extension could constitute the excessive, and therefore dangerous swing that we talked about earlier.

To prevent this, remember to keep your leading shoulder steady and not to swing round with the impetus of the stroke. Remember also to bend your knees when playing this stroke.

LESSON 3
BACKHAND DRIVE

IMPACT
AS WITH THE
FOREHAND DRIVE,
THE WRIST IS
COCKED AND
WEIGHT IS ON THE
LEADING LEG

When I first played squash I found the only way to hit the ball on the backhand side was to use both hands on the racket—I first didn't seem to have the strength to play anything other than a double-handed stroke. British International Paul Millman's father, the Major, gave me my initial basic instruction and insisted that I broke the habit. It was a good decision because in Squash a double-handed stroke is a serious handicap. The backhand is always considered to be the left-hander's weakness and so many of my rivals have attacked that wing over the years that it has been turned into the safest stroke in my repertoire.

During my early competitive days I had developed a steady backhand with the essential ingredient, the open racket face at impact. That very 'open' face caused a cutting action which gave close control but restricted the power content of the stroke. I was especially vulnerable when trying to force the ball past an alert opponent eager to cut off the ball.

As an alternative then to my measured drive I have spent, and will continue to do so, many hours developing more bite and severity on this stroke. I have paid further attention to the cocking of the wrist and the drawing of my left elbow towards my right hip during preparation of the stroke. As the racket comes through to impact, the face is barely open and *at* impact the racket-head is 'coming-up' rather than 'slicing through'.

The main components of the forehand should be seen in the backhand. Remember that the wrist remains 'cocked' throughout and neither breaks during the progress nor after the completion of these strokes. Failing to do this results in an inevitable loss of racket-head and thereby ball-control.

Remember again to keep the leading shoulder steady on the follow-through, thus maintaining further control over the ball and the racket. The latter point will be well appreciated by your opponent !

The footwork, especially when going forwards, will be orthodox (as in the drawing).

LESSON 4
FOREHAND DROPSHOT

THE PERFECT DROP
REBOUNDS INTO
THE SIDEWALL NICK

KEEP THE
WRIST COCKED –
DO NOT FLICK
AT THE BALL

The drop shot is the most delicate stroke in the game and is vital to the armoury of any ambitious player. The perfect drop is one that comes off the front wall and falls in the join between the side wall and floor, the nick.

The last stride into the ball for this stroke should not be too long and uncomfortable nor so short that it restricts one's movement off the foot after completion.

The ball should be struck just in front of the leading foot, the weight being on that foot at the moment of impact.

The racket should come through as for the drive except that the face opens for the impact, thereby cutting the ball, taking the pace off it and making it die sooner.

The follow-through is negligible, perhaps 12 inches, hardly more, and the wrist movement is minimal.

DO NOT on any account break the wrist to flick at the ball.

There are, of course, many types of drop shot—the great Egyptian player Dardir favoured a floated rather than a cut stroke—however, the fundamentals remain constant.

BARRINGTON'S BRUTAL BATTLES 1

THE BREAK-THROUGH

BRITISH OPEN CHAMPIONSHIP		QUARTER FINAL				
DECEMBER 16 1966 LONDON	GAME 1	2	3	4	5	POINTS
JONAH BARRINGTON IRELAND	9	9	8	9		
ABOU TALEB U.A.R.	4	1	10	5		

Taleb, the defending champion, had put on weight. He knew I was being prepared by the Khans to take away his title and Nasrullah, on the day of the match, quietly instilled a mood of confidence in me.

Even in the knock-up Taleb set out to upset me, first by continually hitting the ball to himself and secondly by producing a dazzling array of trick shots. It cost him the match. When the game began he persisted in an exhibition mood. His strokes too frequently hit the tin and I had time to lose my nervousness and to move quietly into a routine of drives and drops. The latter spreadeagled him—too slow into the front of the court, he was unable to make use of his devastating short-game. At two games down and 0–2 in the third Taleb abandoned his hitherto reckless stroke-play for a series of tactics which he pursued with the determination of a rat trying to get off a sinking ship.

He set up, as Rex Bellamy put it, 'a multitude of distractions not the least of them physical intimidation.' He twice changed his shorts and at one stage disappeared from the court for almost ten minutes. At 8–8 in the third, so close to defeat, Taleb conjured up another burst of activity and clawed his way back into the match.

His confidence had now returned and he looked positively jolly after his reprieve in the third, but his slashes for the nick were still intemperate and the mistakes fortunately flowed. Regardless of the incipient tiredness, a dreadful mental weariness, I was determined to knock him off his perch. At 6–6, in the fourth I played the shot which finally broke Taleb's heart—a winning volleyed drop from a shot of his that looked quite irretrievable. The match was mine and the crowd loved the moment of victory almost as much as I.

LESSON 5
BACKHAND DROPSHOT

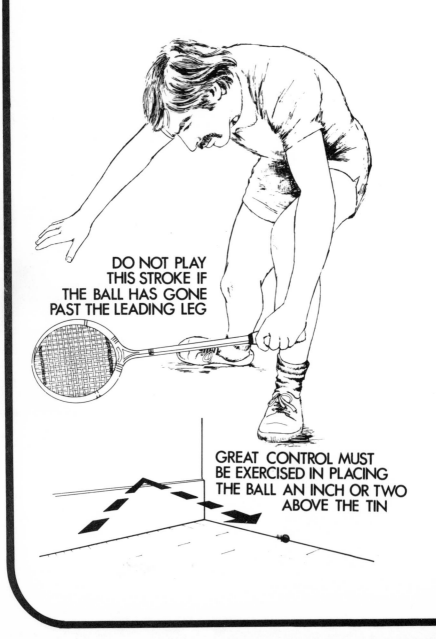

DO NOT PLAY
THIS STROKE IF
THE BALL HAS GONE
PAST THE LEADING LEG

GREAT CONTROL MUST
BE EXERCISED IN PLACING
THE BALL AN INCH OR TWO
ABOVE THE TIN

During my formative years in the game—in other words until today—I have spent many pleasant hours watching one of the world's greatest-ever stroke players, Nasrullah Khan, my coach. He has always insisted that the drop-shot is the 'most beautiful stroke' and 'always my winner when I play it.'

I like to put the opponent behind and then drop the ball from half-court. If the stroke is weak then the enemy still has to cover some distance to reach the ball. When I drop from closer to the front I find the stroke more effective if there is some deception. Merely start the swing as you would for a formal drive and that alone will make him hesitate. When Naz is positioned about the T or near the short or half-court line, with his opponent buried behind him, it is odds on that the wise old Pathan will caress the ball into the nick. He has no such need for deception. He has always taught me to remember that the drop is a brave stroke, played the merest sliver above the tin, and therefore to have everything in my favour before attempting this shot.

The ball must be in a good position so that I can move on to it easily and with perfect balance. If there is any doubt in your mind don't play a drop shot. This is a stroke demanding the greatest control. A placement must be an inch or two above the tin and there is little margin for error.

Never play this stroke when the ball has gone past the leading leg—you are simply asking for trouble. The backhand drop is as for the forehand and is my particular preference. Even if the ball does not slide off the front wall into the side wall nick I try to keep it as close to that side wall as possible, in this way restricting my opponent's return.

An alternative drop shot is the cross court shot. This is very effective when played with delay and most satisfying when the opponent goes the wrong way. Remember, however, to use the variation with discretion, otherwise the vital surprise factor will be missing and the dividend lost.

LESSON 6
FOREHAND VOLLEY

If one considers how frequently the ball is in the air during a rally it is easy to appreciate that the volley is perhaps the most important stroke in the game.

In the early part of my career I volleyed only rarely—I had no confidence nor the habit of doing so—and in letting the ball go past my racket to the back wall, again and again I would let an opponent off the hook. I was allowing him to take, at his ease, the centre of the court, so that I was placed at a disadvantage to the rear.

Tennis players can allow themselves the luxury of a long backswing, but that puts you at a grave disadvantage on a squash court: the short jabbing action, though less elegant, produces the best results and can be the only recourse on a reflex shot.

Whether played high or low, to the back or the front of the court, the most efficient forehand volley is built up on a relatively short back-swing with precious little follow-through after impact. The power comes through wrist and forearm and not the whole arm and shoulder.

KEEP THE FACE OF
THE RACKET SLIGHTLY OPEN

LESSON 7
BACKHAND VOLLEY

'You have a veakness backhand high.' I wonder how many times Azam Khan told me this, and then went on to apply further pressure to that point. The backhand volley, particularly when higher than the shoulder, is extremely difficult to play.

At one time my only reply was to swing my whole body into the ball, almost taking off in my desire to connect. I would then have to try to recover my balance for the next stroke, and against Azam the odds were hopeless.

He taught me that the backhand volley was not the whirling of a scimitar, but a short constructive upwards movement to bring the ball deep, or in a nice concise (as always) cutting action to take it short.

I had to remember to use the forearm strength, not a shoulder movement which costs more effort and provides less control; there should be little follow-through, no swinging round of the body, no breaking of the wrist, no flicking of the ball.

'You have veakness backhand high.'—Indeed most players have. Mine's better now.
Thank you, Azam, for that
and so much more.

USE A 'KARATE CHOP'
ACTION WITH VERY
LITTLE BACKSWING AND
FOLLOW THROUGH

LESSON 8
SERVICE–RIGHT HAND BOX

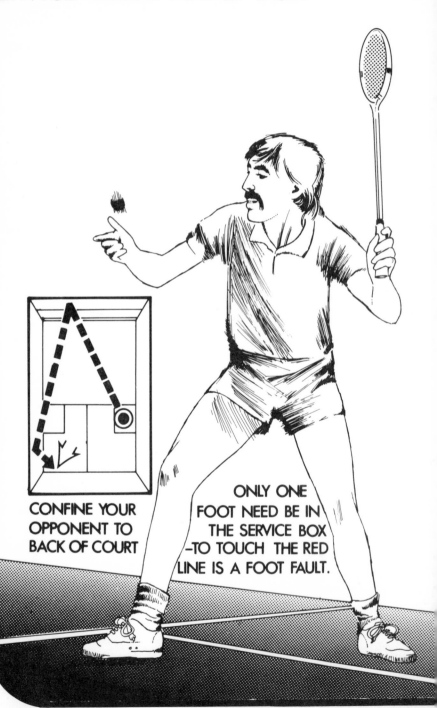

CONFINE YOUR OPPONENT TO BACK OF COURT

ONLY ONE FOOT NEED BE IN THE SERVICE BOX –TO TOUCH THE RED LINE IS A FOOT FAULT.

The importance of a good service needs to be firmly understood; most players of all standards merely use it to put the ball into play, thereby allowing the opponent immediately to come into his own again and take control over the rally.

Remember you have got him where you want him, hesitant, near the back of the court. Be ambitious and go for the outright dividend or at least put him in further difficulty.

First, I place my feet correctly. There is no need for both feet to be in the service-box. I put my right foot outside, comfortably balanced, and the left in the box inside the red line. If it touches the line I am foot faulting so some part of it must remain grounded until the ball has left my racket.

Second, my main service has become nicely grooved because of constant attention to small detail. I like to place a forehand volley lob on to the front wall slightly left of the centre of the court and midway between the cut line and the top red line.

Third, the objective is to serve an outright winner—extremely difficult—or to restrict my opponent's return as much as possible by bringing the ball back off the front wall to hit high on the side wall behind the left service-box. This forces my opponent frequently to hurry his return, especially when the ball is too close to that side wall. If he lets it drop to the rear, he is driven remorselessly into the backhand left corner of the court.

Fourth, after serving with my feet placed correctly, my movement to the centre of the court, the T or just behind it, is very simple and balanced.

Fifth, when the opponent has been shown one's 'grooved' service it does pay to use a variation from time to time. A service straight at him can produce most unexpected success.

LESSON 9
SERVICE–LEFT HAND BOX

PLACE THE FEET TO
MOVE EASILY TO THE
CENTRE OF THE COURT

PLACE THE
BALL WELL UP
ON THE CENTRE
OF THE FRONT
WALL TO MEET
THE SIDE WALL
AS BEFORE

Remember that your service is your one free shot, the one occasion on which you can set your feet with exactitude, briefly examine your opponent's condition, and with the aid of practice and positive thought place the enemy in an even more defensive position.

DO NOT after struggling so demandingly to gain the service then throw it away through sheer carelessness as if it were any unwanted article. You have control, so maintain it through sensible attention to the details already run through in the last lesson. If you are serving a backhand service from the left box the orthodox requirements are the same as for the other side.

However, many left-handed players—and I myself—prefer to serve a forehand service even from the left box. This leaves us briefly with our backs to our opponents (in the drawing you will see both of these services). So ensure first of all that you check your opponent's position before serving. You may be faced with a bit of a crafty devil who could possibly have moved quickly forward to take the ball early, and you, by surprise.

Secondly, ensure that the service is rhythmical and swings you easily to your position on the T or just behind it. A tennis type service will merely take you in on the front wall, reduce your energy and please the opponent considerably.

I place my feet on a line with each other. I prefer a round arm action, just above shoulder height, the ball to be struck well up on the centre of the front wall and again meeting the side wall in the same restrictive area as before.

Remember that when you are serving, or in other words 'in-hand', a point won is a point scored and when you reach nine or ten you will have won the game. In 1968, in the fifth game of the Australian final against Ken Hiscoe, I served three outright winners. Three times I merely had to pick the ball up to go to the other service-box. I wish all my Squash matches were like that! At a lower level a good service will provide an even greater bonus.

LESSON 10
RETURN OF SERVICE

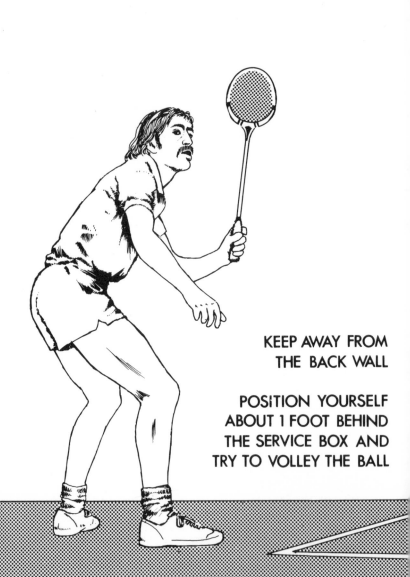

KEEP AWAY FROM
THE BACK WALL

POSITION YOURSELF
ABOUT 1 FOOT BEHIND
THE SERVICE BOX AND
TRY TO VOLLEY THE BALL

The object when returning service is quite simply to place the ball as far away from your opponent as possible. He has taken the centre of the court so the maximum distance he can cover is to a corner.

However it's a bad risk playing the ball to the front corners—hitting the tin means a nice Christmas present and furthermore it is foolish to hit the ball *short* when your opponent is so favourably placed.

The ball should be worked to the back corners, ideally straight down the side wall at varying heights and speeds, but certainly not hit at 100 mph one inch above the tin; this will waste energy and merely place the ball nicely near your opponent on the half-court line.

If you return the ball across the court, whether high or low, remember to play well wide of the T line otherwise the enemy will again gratefully accept the gift.

Do not hang around on the back wall waiting for the service to arrive—it is the one area in the court where you are *most* restricted and you are putting yourself there of your own free-will. Foolish player!

Take a position perhaps a foot behind the outside back corner of the service-box and then you will be in a position to take the ball on the volley—your opponent has therefore less time to settle himself comfortably on the T.

If you are forced backwards, then you should use easy footwork to the rear. *Do not* stare at the front wall—you are not hitting that, I hope!

Keep your eyes on the ball in the server's hand or take in the strength of his swing and movement if he has his back to you. You are the receiver, he is momentarily on top, so compromise—not out of weakness—and aim 95% of your returns at the back corners of the court, dragging him from the T and giving yourself so easily the central position. You are then ready to dominate.

LESSON 11
COMMAND OF THE T POSITION

COMMAND OF THE T POSITION
PLACES YOU ALMOST EQUIDISTANT
FROM THE CORNERS – FROM HERE
YOU CAN STRIKE AT THE BALL
UNDER MOST CIRCUMSTANCES

Domination of the T position provides one of the sure keys to success at Squash. The gradual destruction of an opponent, in great shape before the contest—hair immaculate, complete sartorial elegance—provides me with a profound sense of satisfaction.

As I control from near the centre of the court, the enemy rushes backwards and forwards from corner to corner, ravaged by the immense oxygen debt—unable to breathe —and the lactic acid builds-up in the leg muscles that impairs their function.

I remain supreme in the knowledge that it is I, the matador, a quiet movement here or there, who is reducing the opponent, the bull, to an agonised dribble of over-worked sweat! Nice dream anyway!

Remember that when you are at the T, you are almost equidistant from the four corners of the court, and most balls will be accessible to you. After completing your stroke, don't stand still: hit and then move—to the T. To linger is to lose.

I am frequently and very painfully reminded of the importance of the central position when playing against Geoff Hunt. Like a rat in a trap I am harried from side to side at the back of the court with the accursed Australian calmly clipping his returns to the rear, merely taking a stride off the T and back, before finally sending me on an elephantine progress to the front. In this manner he induces a weak return which again he takes virtually at the T and in an almost bored manner sends me on my way—curse him!

If the beginner, the real rabbit in the club, searches for the T as he plays he will develop one of the most vital habits. When I first played on the American standard court, I instinctively took up my customary position near the T, perhaps just a couple of feet behind, only to find I was quite unable to reach the balls in the front of the court. My incredible slowness really worried me—old age creeping up! My dilemma was happily solved when I finally realised that their T lies much further back in the court. What a quick-witted man am I!

THE COACH

Throughout this manual you will see references to my own coach, Nasrullah Khan. He is so very much a part of my Squash career that any book of mine must have him as an integral part. The coach in all sports has a vital task to fulfill and I shall use Nasrullah's relationship with myself to explain my thinking as to the role I feel he should play.

There are many kinds of coaches and most of them are regrettably suspect in some respect. Before anyone can be qualified to tutor to a very high level, he must be aware of the many diverse problems that beset the pupil. He can only *understand* these difficulties if he has suffered them himself.

Technique can be transferred from coach to pupil by theory. There have been many excellent technical coaches in Squash who have not achieved international playing success (Alan McClausland and Brian Boys who masterminded Hunt's technique and expertise when Geoff was in his teens).

In my view Nasrullah has an incomparable technique and capacity for imparting his knowledge if his pupil is worthy of it. I was fortunate that I had someone to copy and would spend hours watching him play his drop-shot —deadly—and other strokes. He always contrived to make me realise that every stroke he played was the result of years of assiduous individual practice—making the stroke grooved and automatic and the mind clear as to the successful outcome.

The coach in Squash must mould many pieces together until he makes his pupil into an exciting whole. Not only must he determine the areas of advancement on the court, but he must provide his pupil with an additional variation of work away from his cell, and give him a philosophy which does not stifle, but makes him realise that self-discipline is inherent in any really successful sporting prospect and that moderation in everything but training is a must.

Nasrullah provided me with a comprehensive routine which demanded complete dedication and, because of my relatively dissolute past, an extreme acceptance of discipline, which confined me to the atmosphere of Squash and no other social environment. *I* needed a drastic overhaul, whereas *my pupils* on the whole are much more mature in their thinking and can appreciate the need for 'commonsense' in everything. Every pupil is different but the common denominator is the wholehearted willingness to undertake a daily habit of hard work—the lambs are soon sorted out.

The true coach draws up a programme for his pupil embracing work on the court, the playing and practice side. If he can work with his pupil, all the better—it *is* easier to respect someone who applies practicalities instead of eternal theory. There should be off-court variation in training—to improve strength in a particular area and for general conditioning. The coach must know where to send his pupil for specialised work such as weights—in that area professional supervision is very necessary.

However skilful the coach may be in imparting the theory of technique and simple tactics, unless he has himself been involved in the playing of the game at a high level he cannot fully understand the mental stresses which occur both before, during and after championship encounters. How can a man win his fifth British Open and be enormously depressed? The coach has to be aware of so many trials and tribulations and then be able to offer a reasonable remedy. So frequently he has to be almost overbearing in motivating his protégé and yet so sensitive when dealing with personal problems.

At some stage the coach-pupil relationship must change. The disciple himself becomes an acknowledged master of his art and then there may be an area of aggravation. The coach wants to retain his absolute authority and is jealous of any possible interference—Freud can explain that one better!—but the boy has grown into a man and a compromise must be made. If he has been taught well, he will be capable of enormous dedication without word of command and yet he should know that the coach is always there to advise and to correct his game.

His mentor's role must now be a subsidiary but a proud one.

LESSON 12
RACKET HEAD UP

KEEP THE RACKET HEAD ABOVE THE
LEVEL OF THE WRIST

If you were to walk around with your playing wrist permanently bent backwards you would definitely short-cut your way to successful stroke play. However, this might make you a little conspicuous and many of your closest friends might think your behaviour a trifle strange.

It is undoubtedly far more natural and comfortable to hang the head of the racket downwards after completion of a stroke. Like everybody else, even three years ago, I trailed my racket almost to the floor as I waited at the T or sped after the ball.

Time and again when it would have paid me to volley, I just did not have enough time in which to bring my racket up, back, and then complete even my short swing.

All the British players seemed to suffer from the same disease, although I must confess it didn't seem to bother *them* much: but the top Australians, always positive in their approach, tried to remedy this natural defect and Hunt and Hiscoe especially have succeeded.

Both cut off the ball constantly and can do so because at the completion of their strokes they do not allow the wrist to break. By keeping it cocked the racket head is kept on or above the level of the wrist and is, in fact, already in the striking position to be drawn back for a drive, volley, or drop.

In the drawing it will be clearly seen that I am in a position to move to play any stroke and my racket is nestling nicely in front of me. I find that I can now take an earlier ball more effectively because of this automatic and more economical movement.

The racket only needs to be brought just above the level of the wrist. I had one most enthusiastic pupil who was determined to master the habit and at every opportunity waved the racket well above his head. This was a stirring sight but of little value as he then reverted to his old habit as he prepared to swing. Down would go the racket-head to the ground, then panic would overtake him as the ball was rapidly gaining the advantage and an amazing further whirring would take place in the hope that contact would be made. At least he tried!

LESSON 13
THE CROUCH

THE SUPPLE POSTURE
OF THE CROUCH – LEGS APART
THE BODY BENT AT THE BACK AND KNEES

Hashim Khan was the champion of champions; there can be no dispute over that. At the same time his younger brother Azam maintains that *he* had a much more exact drop shot then Hashim and his volleys were better. Yet he then assures me that his brother always gave him a seven point start in practice and beat him! How could that happen?

Hashim moved faster than any other player, so speedy was he that one British opponent smelt burning rubber when the wretched man sped past him! He could never have been called an elegant player as he crouched bowlegged and barrel-chested assessing the opponent's move before he finally pounced.

There is no doubt that to be really successful at Squash one needs to have a little of the animal in one's nature— perhaps in appearance as well! To move quickly in a small area a player must not adopt too upright a stance. The splendid guardsman on duty at the T will just remain splendidly static when he needs to spring after the ball.

The Squash player should adopt a cat-like posture on his toes, legs comfortably apart, bending the back and the knees. My brother swears I'm on the payroll of the osteopaths, but I can assure you that if you can persevere albeit gently, with this position, not only will there be no need for medical aid, but your squash will improve considerably.

It is no excuse to say you are too big to crouch. Ken Hiscoe, the great Australian, does just that more effectively than any of his contemporaries, and he is a large man. Our diagram shows that this position is accentuated when waiting at the T, but also emphasises the same supple bending of the body when playing a low ball or when uncoiling like a snake to strike at a high one. Try it—I do.

LESSON 14
THE LONG STRIDE

The long stride, which has been called the *Barrington Gobble* is the most effective way to move in the game. Hashim Khan, Abou Taleb, and Dick Carter immediately spring to mind as men who have employed this method. With a couple of long strides these men, all small, have eaten up the squash-court.

Less proficient players quite probably use shorter steps, a pitter-patter movement which just does not stand up to the pressure of top class Squash. But it is not just the top-class competitor who benefits from using the gobbling stride—any average club player with a little concentration on this area will find his game improves.

Because his movement to the ball is better, so will be his balance on striking and also, very important, his movement away from his opponent's path and back to the T position. Little steps restrict: none of the great players who teach—and they do know—will advocate that. Nasrullah always advises 'You must move with a long, long stride.' Cultivate at least a long last stride to the ball—gobble, gobble, gobble.

LESSON 15
LENGTH

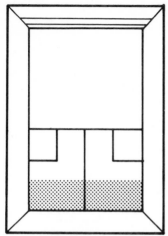

FIRST BOUNCE

DEAD NICK

THE LENGTH IS THE STROKE WHICH SENDS THE BALL TO THE BACK OF THE COURT – A PERFECT LENGTH SENDS THE BALL ON ITS SECOND BOUNCE INTO THE NICK (JOIN BETWEEN FLOOR AND WALL)

Length is what the game of Squash is all about. It constitutes the most important feature of the game and provides not only the outright dividend, the winner, but more certainly, the simple foundation to almost every winning stroke.

The 'perfect length' is a ball struck either high or low, hard or slow, to the back of the court, so that on the second bounce it catches the join between the floor and the back wall—the dead nick—and no arguments about that. This is the ultimate reward, but otherwise a 'good length' is a ball struck to the back of the court, which forces the opponent to the one area where he is most restricted and inhibited in his stroke play.

In the Drive diagrams the best length to the back of the court is clearly shown—the ball hitting the dead nick. At the same time the restrictive area is also shown; one can see also that a good length ball is one which is driven down the wall but in fact catches the wall behind the service-box area, thereby losing pace and angling off that wall into the back of the court.

Good length gives you control of the T and allows you to seize on any weak return from behind, and then to play your dazzling array of just-above-the-tin-winners.

LESSON 16
EYE ON THE BALL

HAVING GAINED CONTROL OF THE
T POSITION MAKE SURE YOU KNOW
WHAT'S GOING ON BEHIND YOUR BACK

ALWAYS KEEP YOUR EYE ON THE BALL
WHETHER IT IS IN FRONT OR BEHIND YOU

There is a classic character in Squash called 'the front wall starer.' He it is who strikes the ball majestically to the back of the court, driving his opponent to the rear, and then, having settled himself comfortably in command on the T, promptly undoes the greater part of his hitherto good work by neglecting to keep his head turned so that his eyes can, like a hawk, trace the course of the ball.

His eyes are pinned to that front wall. But why? What can he see that escapes me? Beautiful though it first may be to the beholder surely he must at some time grow tired of peering at it.

I now must make a confession. I too was once contaminated. In trying to kick the habit I found for one month my game only deteriorated, but that was only because I was spending so much time reminding myself of what *not* to do, that I was still quite unable to react positively.

However, through perseverance I survived and the momentous day finally arrived when I joyfully saw the ball onto and off my opponent's racket. Nasrullah trained me to follow the ball wherever it might be in the court, even after it had hit a dead nick and when I couldn't get within half a court of it.

Remember that by keeping your eyes on the ball it is easier for your brain to transmit the necessary early signal that another stroke has to be played, should the ball be returned. Never mind whether you have instant reflexes, eyes should always be on the ball (even when it is behind you) and taking in your opponent's swing. Throughout my career I have suffered spells when my ball control and general play have become quite appalling. The diagnosis and remedy are inevitably the same—that I have become sloppy and am not concentrating on this one fundamental. Once aware of the fault, I give myself the necessary prescription. All of us must watch that little black ball— not the front wall, not just the man.

LESSON 17
WHEN BEHIND OPPONENT

Place ball on cut   Between cut and tin   Well above cut

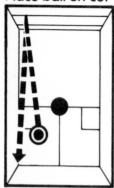 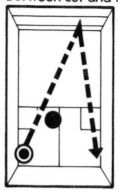 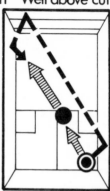

FOLLOW STROKE—DON'T STAND STILL—LESSEN THE OPPONENT'S ANGLE OF DEEP RETURN

I am often asked about tactics (more often than not about what to do when behind an opponent). If the discussion develops, the content becomes more complicated. Nasrullah and Azam by word of mouth and practical example taught me a very simple, uncomplicated method *in theory.*

In practice, the successful application of the theory demands tremendous concentration and discipline. But some method is essential and fundamental to any successful game. If during the course of a match you seem to see little else than the opponent's bottom, then, believe me, you are going to be the loser.

When you are buried behind an opponent dominating the T position there can only be two basic replies—after you accept the fact that for the moment he is on top and you are at a disadvantage.

A sensible compromise is called for with a calculated objective—to play the ball either down the side wall or across the court, as in two of our diagrams, ensuring that it carries to one of the back corners, thereby displacing the opponent to the rear and achieving for yourself easy movement to the T and control over the rally.

Ninety percent of the time when behind, play the return deep, placing the ball near to or above the cut line (i.e. the service line on the front wall) to bring the ball past the opponent.

There is little in your favour, so precious little point in playing the ball short about one or two inches above the tin—the odds are against all of us in that situation.

There are variations of course, but these should be used with considerable discretion. Where the opponent is tiring, not looking behind (a front wall starer), or on his heels, then the boast (angle), long drop or reverse angle can be most effective. If possible first show him the pattern to the back of the court; it is a principle to be observed not only by world champions but the real rabbits in your clubs.

Another useful tip is to remember that the more restricted you are, basically the higher and slower should be your return on the front wall. When tied up in the back corners close to the side wall it is silly to attempt to hit the ball out hard. There will tend to be greater inaccuracy and the ball will go back to the grateful enemy that much quicker, perhaps even before you have really had time to move off your stroke.

It is so much better to give the ball slow height which at least gives you time to move out of torture territory back to the T. Your opponent has to wait for that ball and the delay is vital. Should you be quite unable to play that stroke, don't try to escape by attempting to hit a low fast boast just a couple of inches above the tin. That is a foolish gamble and doomed to failure in the long run.

I have been taught to play a slow high boast out, which again my opponent has to wait for as it lingers in the air, and I move insidiously up behind him. Also I use the back-wall boast for this same purpose.

LESSON 18
WHEN IN FRONT OF OPPONENT

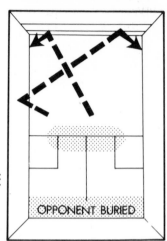

OPPONENT BURIED

WHEN IN CONTROL OF THE
T & PERFECTLY BALANCED –
THIS IS THE TIME TO PLAY
THE BALL SHORT

Recently I took time out to watch Nasrullah put a particularly cocky young player in his place. He had upset Naz by insisting that they should play rather than have the old maestro teach him a few tricks. The game lasted fourteen minutes and the score to the wily warrior was 9–0, 9–0, 9–0. Throughout he remained completely unperturbed and gently took up a lease on the T and played approximately two strokes—the lob which took the opponent back, and on the occasion when the ball running down the back wall was somehow miraculously returned, the drop shot to the front which usually nicked. Sometimes as boredom set in and he felt perhaps his balance wasn't quite perfect, Nasrullah rejected his drop shot in favour of yet another lob which further deflated the puffed-up pride of the young rooster.

Yet again I was given a practical reminder by my old teacher that the best fundamental tactic in Squash is to get in front of your opponent—perfectly in control of the centre of the court—and to have him scuttling like a harassed bunny behind you. When he plays a satisfyingly weak return from a particularly unfavourable position, and this is very, very clearly shown in our diagram, then comes your opportunity to play your stroke to the front of the court—a drop shot, short volley, angle or hard hit kill.

BARRINGTON'S BRUTAL BATTLES 2

CONSOLIDATION AND THE DOUBLE

BRITISH AMATEUR CHAMPIONSHIP						FINAL
JANUARY 16 1967 LONDON	GAME 1	2	3	4	5	POINTS
JONAH BARRINGTON IRELAND	1	9	7			4
DICK CARTER AUSTRALIA	9	6	9			7

Dick Carter, the celebrated 'Ant' started in a hurry. He calmly harried me round the court and into considerable error. I hit the tin with methodical persistence and rapidly found myself a game down and very ill at ease. At 2–5 in the second I began at last to get to grips with the 'Ant' and started to worm my way back into the match.

The second game was hard fought, many long rallies, tremendous retrieving, but I was home at 9–6. The third was perilously close, but I sensed the longer the game went on the better my rhythm was becoming. Yet at 7–6 I fell into error again. Carter read the mood well, and increased the pressure to take a two games to one lead.

He was now in full flight, and I seemed mentally eroded. He refused to make any errors and also hit a magnificent length. But at 7–4 Carter was as close as he would ever be to the Amateur Championship.

Then ensued one of the most critical rallies of my career—almost throughout holding the whip-hand, he finally drew me wide on the right, collected a weak cross-court return and struck his 'winner'. But the ball clipped the top of the tin—so near yet so far. In the words of Rex Bellamy: 'It was enough; Barrington, showing the resilience of a great competitor, swept through to two games all. But the fifth game, incredibly, was over in less than four minutes. Carter was weary. He tried to hit two winners. Both went down. His stamina had been broken and he could never get a rally going again. With four winners of his own and five errors by Carter, Barrington romped through that last game in one hand. For the second time in 27 days, the champagne was flowing in Berkeley Square.'

LESSON 19
INDIVIDUAL PRACTICE–DRIVE

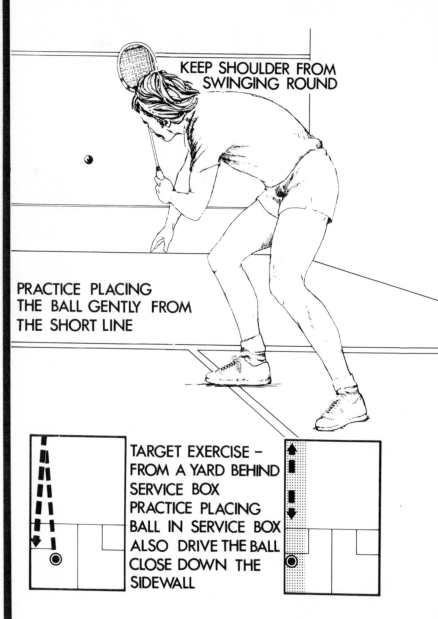

KEEP SHOULDER FROM SWINGING ROUND

PRACTICE PLACING THE BALL GENTLY FROM THE SHORT LINE

TARGET EXERCISE – FROM A YARD BEHIND SERVICE BOX PRACTICE PLACING BALL IN SERVICE BOX ALSO DRIVE THE BALL CLOSE DOWN THE SIDEWALL

I can never over-emphasise the importance of individual practice—that is working out on your own. Whatever your standard, top-class competitor or social rabbit, a real way to make a substantial improvement is by self-practice. All my basic individual practices were developed for me by Nasrullah Khan. I remember him taking me to the court to practise the forehand and backhand drives and breaking this exercise into three stages.

1. To hit the ball repetitively against the front wall from the short line. My proximity to the front wall prevented me from hitting the ball hard. In placing the ball gently I was able to concentrate on the position of my feet, orthodox racket swing and keeping the shoulders from sweeping round, thereby preventing me from pulling the ball off line and across the court.

2. To come a yard behind the service-box, and still remembering the points above, to see how many times consecutively I could slot the ball into the service-box without error—a target exercise.

3. To play the ball down the side wall as close to it as possible, varying the pace of the stroke, high and slow, hard and lower to the back, and very tight to the tin when hitting short for a kill. It gave me the confidence to do just this during a match, and it took away the inherent fear of playing such a stroke and making a dreadful mess of it.

This last practice, like the others for both the forehand and backhand drives, has enabled me to be completely at ease when hitting the ball down the wall. Those players who have never practised regularly are always wary when the ball is even as much as a foot off the wall. Because they haven't done the practice they tend to prefer to hit the ball across the court and too often give an opponent a chance to really capitalise. The 'clinger' down the wall is the best stroke in the game—nobody applauds this unspectacular stroke, but my word, how it frustrates the opposition!

LESSON 20
INDIVIDUAL PRACTICE–VOLLEY

FROM THE SHORT LINE PLAY CONSECUTIVE FOREHAND OR BACKHAND VOLLEYS AGAINST THE CUT LINE

APPROX 6ft

PRACTICE PLAYING REPEATED VOLLEYS AGAINST THE FRONT WALL WITH A 'KARATE CHOP' ACTION

If the ball is not on the ground, then it must be in the air and this means you are required to play the volley. One day, six years ago, when I already fancied my chances, Nasrullah Khan assured me I volleyed like a baby and therefore that I had to start to learn the stroke at kindergarten level.

Because he wanted me to develop a short automatic swing, so different from tennis, he brought me within six feet of the front wall and told me simply to try to keep playing successive volleys from that position. I thought I would teach 'the old fool' a lesson and casually played one. By the time my racket had come through again, the ball had shot past. The ace head-shrinker had done his job well! So I was forced to swing short, almost a jab, or karate chop, and soon learned that whenever I used this stroke, this action was the most successful.

A good general practice is to place yourself (as is shown in the diagram) on the short line and to see how many consecutive forehand or backhand volleys you can play without error against or near the cut-line on the front wall. This week your world record may be five, so next week the target will be ten. Don't crack the ball high on the front wall, don't cheat yourself, be disciplined in your practice and this will be transferred into your matches.

The footwork for this practice can be orthodox or unorthodox. In a game of Squash one must be capable of playing the ball off either foot and very often, particularly when going sideways or backwards on the forehand side, it pays to strike off what too many coaches call the 'wrong foot'. As I have said before, the player who has command in the air can frighten off so many opponents with greater speed and better ground-strokes.

I have already emphasised the need to volley, if possible, on return of service. Most players do find it difficult to strike the ball above shoulder level. I will give you another good exercise to overcome this weakness. Place yourself in the return of service position and then play high consecutive volleys down the same side wall. Practice does improve this and every other stroke.

LESSON 21
INDIVIDUAL PRACTICE-DROPSHOT

PRACTICE FROM IN FRONT OF THE T POSITION – PLACE THE BALL JUST ABOVE TIN TO GLIDE INTO THE SIDEWALL NICK.

If you're not hitting the ball deep, then you should be bringing it short, perhaps using your drop-shot. The object with this stroke is to place the ball just above the tin so that it then angles down into the join between the side wall and floor, the nick. That, of course, is the outright winner and frequently one has to settle for second best which is to bring the ball off the front wall and running close to, and down, the side wall.

Place yourself first in front of the T, gently hit the ball at about the height of the cut line on the front wall and near the side wall, so that it is now coming back towards you. Move in on the ball, weight on the front foot at the moment of the impact which will occur about six inches in front of the leading foot. Keep the face of the racket open, thereby cutting and slicing the ball to take the pace off and make it die more easily.

Do not break the wrist or flick or follow through more than 12 inches beyond impact—otherwise the effect will be lost. I like to make my last stride into the ball long, so giving me an unrestricted stroke and, most important, easy movement out of my opponent's path to the ball.

LESSON 22
THE BOAST AND VOLLEY-BOAST

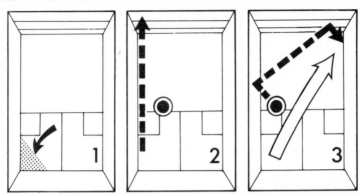

THE VOLLEY-BOAST, A VITAL ATTACKING STROKE
1. THE OPPONENT IS BURIED.   2. HE RETALIATES
WITH A FAST RETURN DOWN THE WALL.
3. THE VOLLEY-BOAST (OFF SIDE WALL, ACROSS
FRONT WALL, LOW OVER TIN TO OPPOSITE SIDE
WALL) KEEPS YOUR OPPONENT ON THE MOVE.

The boast and volley boast are unquestionably two of the most excellent attacking strokes.

I find I gain my best results with these shots when I have played my opponent deep. A fast return from my opponent, which I anticipate, is played down the wall. I then hit the ball flat onto the side wall, drawing it across the face of the front wall, low over the tin and dragging in onto the opposite side wall; this takes the opponent, fractionally static after his hard hit return, on a hectic charge across the court.

Geoff Hunt and Ken Hiscoe have the confidence to play the boast regularly from behind the opponent. Their stroke is not exceptionally hard and tends to drift nastily off and close to the front wall—Hunt's even more slowly than Hiscoe's. They then follow the opponent in and wait around the T to pounce on any weak reply. Most players have neither the talent nor the movement to achieve such success.

Again both boasts can be played off either foot but when going forward the orthodox position is preferable and the ball will be struck almost parallel to the body, up onto the side wall to come on a downward trajectory onto and off the front wall.

LESSON 23
THE LOB

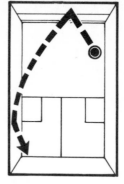

THE LOB IS A USEFUL STROKE FOR GAINING TIME – SEND THE BALL WELL UP INTO THE AIR, TO STRIKE THE SIDE WALL BEHIND THE SERVICE BOX & CONFINE YOUR OPPONENT TO THE BACK OF THE COURT

The lob is the most underestimated stroke in the game. Except for the times I have betrayed my training—and have attempted to ape the more attractive but less effective strokes of many of my rivals—I have religiously applied, in championship play, a methodical game in which the lob plays an integral role as both an offensive and defensive measure (the last is well shown in the diagram). It is the great rhythm-breaker and complement to the short, low strokes.

When I'm in trouble in the front of the court, or indeed whenever I'm in a spot of difficulty I will give the ball as much air as possible, lobbing well up into the lights (!) and especially to my opponent's backhand side, since very few players can handle a forceful high backhand return. This at least gives me a small amount of time to recover to the T position.

Whether suddenly lobbing to change the pace, driving my opponent to the preserve at the rear, or as a desperate defensive measure, I try to bring the ball into the side wall just beyond the back of the service-box area, thus taking any pace off the stroke and confining the ball even more securely to the back of the court.

My old practice-partner, Jonathan Smith, another English International, was a great exponent of this stroke. Whenever in trouble he would lift the ball to the heavens and defy me to kill as it travelled insidiously down from the rafters. At another time he would move smoothly into the forecourt, beautifully balanced, racket-face nicely open, obviously about to play one of his unsporting drops; then, instead of cutting the ball short, he would maliciously use that now very open face to lift the ball over the advancing Barrington. Blast him! I never could read that perverse stroke, but at least I've tried to copy it!

BARRINGTON'S BRUTAL BATTLES 3

FALL FROM GRACE

WORLD AMATEUR CHAMPIONSHIP							
AUGUST 24 1967	MELBOURNE	GAME 1	2	3	4	5	POINTS
JONAH BARRINGTON IRELAND		7	6	7			
CAM NANCARROW AUSTRALIA		9	9	9			

My journey to the other side of the globe for the first ever official World Amateur Championship quickly brought me back to earth and was a severe lesson that there was so much to learn.

On arrival in Sydney with the British team I had struggled from the start and suffered shatteringly swift defeats from Hiscoe and Nancarrow. I found myself in an abysmal slough of which the name was despond and I had almost convinced myself I would never adapt to the Australian ball, let alone win with it against their best players. However, a week of success in the Queensland Championships, and seven days of therapy with my great friend Aub Amos in Brisbane, brought my confidence and ambition back.

I returned to Sydney, just lost a great struggle with Hiscoe in the Test series and despatched the rest of my opponents quite efficiently. The scene was now all set for Melbourne and the Individual Title, for which I was seeded 1. In the semi-final I was due to meet Carter again and Hiscoe found Hunt opposite him. But Cameron Nancarrow, who was seeded No. 5, clearly had other ideas. He disposed of Dick Carter in a memorable quarter-final and I was now faced by a man who, over a period of time, was to earn the nickname 'Jonah's Jinx'. I had played the tall young left-hander some twenty months before in London and overcame him in four. He had played indifferently but nearly pulled himself out of trouble in the fourth and I fear would have gone on to win in five. I was not confident of success and certainly didn't look forward to the encounter.

My fears were not dispelled. I was never on terms once the first game had begun. He struck the ball tremendously hard, pinned me in the back corners and pressured me into playing drop-shots from behind when just not positioned well enough. Unless the stroke was accurate he proved far too deceptive when playing round the front of the court and out of desperation I narrowed my margin and inevitably hit the tin with monotonous regularity. Nancarrow's aggression took him to 6–2 in the first game, but briefly I came back at him, although it was due more to a wavering in his concentration than to any quality play on my part. I reached 6–7 before he gathered himself again to take the game and he then roared away in seemingly unstoppable fashion to an 8–3 lead in the second. Again I flattered only to deceive and he was at 9–6, two games ahead and going with the wind.

Now I was fighting for my life, but still without much pattern. Ambition is a powerful persuader and the fear of defeat can also unleash one to greater labour. I led, for the first time, at 5–3 but it was not enough. Nancarrow seemed to be slowing a little, but his box of tricks remained inexhaustible and he added to my considerable frustration by his total reluctance to take his giraffe-like body out of the way after striking the ball.

I spent too much time giving the referee the evil eye, but he seemed to be totally unaware of the predicament and my appeals fell on stony ground. The dreaded 'Lurch' advanced to 8–5 and at this juncture I staved off five bitterly fought match points before finally succumbing to a drop-shot which was apparently good. I spent a second trying to reach it by climbing through Cam's legs and ended up pathetically lying on the floor appealing for a let, but mercy came there none!

There could be no complaint, regardless of any other factors. Cam Nancarrow had clearly played the best squash and on the day proved himself the better player. We were to join battle again and controversy seemed a constant companion to our clashes.

BARRINGTON'S BRUTAL BATTLES 4
THE BRINK

WORLD TEAM SERIES							
FEBRUARY 10 1969 NOTTINGHAM	GAME 1	2	3	4	5	POINTS	
JONAH BARRINGTON IRELAND	2	9	4	9		3	
AFTAB JAWAID PAKISTAN	9	5	9	3		8	

The most important event in amateur squash came to Britain in early 1969. The International Championships were held at a multitude of centres ending with the Individual Amateur World Title at the Lansdowne Club. The Team Series was based at Edgbaston Priory Club in Birmingham. The British team was proving quite effective and, by February 10th, was in a position to challenge the favourites Australia, in the final match. But Pakistan still lay in the path and there is many a slip . . . !

Paul Millman, at No. 3 lost fairly comprehensively in the opening match to the 18 year old Alauddin. First blood to the Pakistanis. The pressure was really on, as Aftab Jawaid, three times British Amateur champion, and I took the court. We had faced each other only once before in competition, two long years before, when I beat him in the Open Championship final. He had always been exceedingly introverted just before a match, detaching himself to sit quietly pondering the struggle ahead. However, this time his tactics were very different—he was positively effervescent and obviously relaxed as if unaware of the importance of the occasion. I should have been wary for his mind is always boldly calculating, but I was still raw and in this case ruthlessly deceived.

From the outset Jawaid was masterfully efficient, his trademark throughout his illustrious career. For long periods he played a tight game to perfection. His length was immaculate and his drop-shot never sharper. In comparison I felt terribly tense and ill at ease. Four silly mistakes in the first game and Jawaid remorselessly took the lead.

The second game was scrappy, for my part, but I managed to keep my volleys and drops above the tin after placing him deep to the rear backhand corner. In the third he again slipped into a winning lead.

In the fourth, although the cunning Aftab had again been almost jocular in the interval between the games, my own discipline returned. Desperation is a considerable spur and I was never in any danger once the lead had been taken. So after sixty minutes play the match was delicately balanced and tension now ran very high in the gallery.

Jawaid had little to say at this stage but he rapidly expressed his authority in the fifth and I trailed 1–6. I was now in a perilous situation which was marginally reduced by two winners—score 3–6. Aftab took advantage of another dreadful error from me and stood arrogantly at 8–3, match point, not only for him but also for Pakistan. It was a grim moment.

We then played a rally which seemed to begin in one era and end in another. It was terminated by a let.

Suddenly Jawaid seemed to feel at last the burden he too was carrying and perhaps unwisely decided to end his labour in haste. He went for winners uncharacteristically and hit down three forehands. Strangely I now had him on the run—he wasn't exhausted but mentally he was broken and didn't really believe he could win.

He failed to serve again as I stormed through to take the game and match 10–8. His discipline had gone, his resolution lay suddenly far away and Great Britain was back in the series. The last game had taken thirty-seven minutes—it was worth it.

BARRINGTON'S BRUTAL BATTLES 5
ECLIPSE

WORLD AMATEUR CHAMPIONSHIP						
FEBRUARY 26 1969 LONDON	GAME 1	2	3	4	5	POINTS
JONAH BARRINGTON IRELAND	7	9				3
GEOFF HUNT AUSTRALIA	9	2				0

On the morning of February 26th 1969, Rex Bellamy wrote in *The Times*:— 'Jonah Barrington, a 27 year old Cornishman who has reminded British sportsmen that dedicated hard work is the only currency that can buy success, today plays his last squash rackets match as an amateur. He meets Geoff Hunt (Victoria) in the final of the World Championship at the Lansdowne Club, London. The Duke of Edinburgh will present the prizes.'

It was one of the real moments of truth. I had laid down the gauntlet over a period of eighteen months and had won title after title. Six national championships came my way. I had faltered in the British Open a month earlier, but my ultimate target all along the road had been the World Amateur Championship. It had proved to be a memorable competition and my game had been, if not spectacular, at least competently reassuring. In the semi-finals Hunt had laid Hiscoe low after a violently enthralling match and in contrast I had finally beaten Cam Nancarrow. Indeed such was my concentration that I led 9–0 and 5–0 before my 'Jinx' got off the mark. I felt unbelievable relief after I had run out 10–8 in an excruciatingly close third game.

Both Nasrullah and Azam told me to concentrate my attack on Hunt's backhand, to be eternally patient and to erode him mentally in a long first game. The first rally lasted for over three minutes and I led 4–0 after twelve minutes playing to the precise pattern. Geoff was not hitting as hard as he had in previous encounters; as it turned out he had sensibly decided to pace himself in the hot atmosphere of the Bruce Court. My early break made me incautious and I relapsed into errors as I struck for ill-calculated winners. It was a close affair but Hunt was home at 9–7.

In the second I not only contained him but started to move him from corner to corner. He was doing a lot of work and he didn't like it. He seemed to lack fire throughout and I was able to control the pace to level the match and then surge into a 3–0 lead in the third. Geoff really seemed to be tiring and I suddenly began to scent victory.

I was building my castle on quicksand and lost the day at this very moment. He knew he was going to lose unless his tactics were changed. His calculation was simple. If Barrington was going to take the title then Barrington would have to win every single point—he would not make unforced errors to help him on his way.

Not only did Geoff Hunt not make another error throughout the match, but he also imposed his game on me. His length was superb and he now employed his back-hand boast to take me short. I was rattled, my defences scattered. The third was his, 9–3 and the fourth followed the same remorseless pattern.

There were no chinks in his armour and I was drawn in the end into the trap of hitting out of desperation with no reason behind the strokes. Inevitably, as his game became even more confident and assured, so mine grew in hopeless inaccuracy. Twice I ran across the lines and twice I paid the full penalty. Geoff Hunt finally sealed my fate to clinch the World Amateur Title for the second time.

LESSON 24
THE NICK

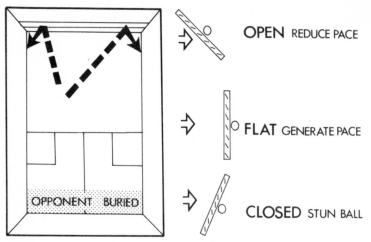

OPEN REDUCE PACE

FLAT GENERATE PACE

CLOSED STUN BALL

OPPONENT BURIED

The nick stroke can be played off the ground or in the air—the object being to place the ball with exactitude in the join between the floor and a side wall (a dead nick) or almost doing the same (half nick). This is the kill of kills and can be played with delicacy or power. More often than not, because of little attention to practice and position, this stroke either hits the tin or sets the ball up for the enemy.

Again my advice is first to ensure that the opponent has been uncomfortably displaced to the rear, that the ball is then taken early (and with reassuring composure) and then at least there is a possibility that the stroke will succeed. A few hundred hours' practice of this shot on your own will pay a rather surer dividend! On the forehand side I hit this shot flat; on the backhand I use a great deal of cut unless, on the ground stroke, I can take the ball well above the tin. Then I try to win the point with a stroke played with a flat or closed racket and hit at about a 100 miles an hour!

The nick is also found at the back of the court and one of the best strokes is the length ball which drives into the nick just beyond the back of the service-boxes. Hashim Khan was the original exponent of the nick kill in the front of the court. He grew bored after a couple of years of hanging about and decided one day to finish the rallies sooner rather than later!

LESSON 25
RACKET HEAD UP (ADVANCED)

Most players fail to keep the head of the racket up after completion of their shots—the wrist breaks result in an obviously less effcient shot production. Another prime fault is that of actually *arriving* at the ball and then having to draw the racket back.

Power is definitely gained by striking the ball as the weight comes down on the leading foot. If the racket head is brought back early to preparation position behind the head, there will be less tendency to rush the stroke. I wish I had learned this at the beginning.

Geoff Hunt has very obviously worked hard to cultivate the right habit. He arrives at the ball with the racket head right back behind his head and his opponents would swear on the Bible—or Koran—that he is about to unleash a thunderbolt. Suddenly, the racket goes through and the most delicate drop-shot or angle is produced. Of course it's all luck!

**GET THE RACKET HEAD UP EARLY
AS YOU MOVE TO THE BALL**

LESSON 26
RETRIEVING WIDE INTO SIDEWALLS

UPWARD STROKE — BELOW CUT

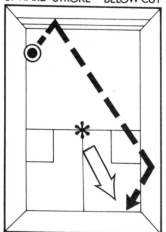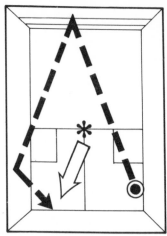

WHEN UNDER PRESSURE DRIVE THE BALL WIDE OF THE T, STRIKE THE SIDEWALL AND DRAW YOUR OPPONENT TO THE BACK OF THE COURT

Most players when under pressure in the front of the court return the ball as best they can to the back. This is what I would want to do myself—following the fundamental rule that when in difficulty, hit the ball deep rather than try a risky short stroke. Remember with a short stroke the odds are stacked against you.

The classic, and in fact instinctive, retrieving stroke is across court rather than straight down the wall. I must have lost a thousand points in my career because of a basic weakness in my thinking when playing this stroke. I don't want my pupils to make the same error—they are taught to 'think wide' as in the two diagrams.

Never aim directly for the corner of the court—that will take the ball across the T and *there* will possibly be your opponent—curtains. Aim to bring the ball into the side wall first—the perfect shot being the one where the ball hits the side wall nick at the back of the service-box. You will at least move your opponent backwards from the central position and give yourself the most valuable fraction of time to regain that position yourself. When deep in the mire, 'think wide', 'hit high' and pray!

LESSON 27
'WRONG' FOOT

When going forwards to strike the ball, try to get your feet placed correctly—right foot leading for the forehand and left for the backhand. However, when forced backwards I have learned, to work off what the textbook coaches have called the 'wrong' foot. My Australian adversary, Geoff Hunt, is the best exponent of this technique. He keeps cropping up, doesn't he? Anyway try it for yourselves.

Hit the ball to the back of the court—forehand side—and then move to it, placing your right foot leading towards the corner. The only stroke you can play satisfactorily from that position is a boast, and look how difficult it is to move back to the centre of the court after completion—your body is locked.

Now hit the ball to the same area, left foot leading towards the corner, and besides having room for almost totally unrestricted hitting, there is an immense advantage in freedom of movement as well. The method is also successful when moving sideways to take the ball. It is more difficult on the backhand side, but nevertheless has paid a handsome dividend for Geoff and myself—a reasonable recommendation. Remember that these instructions are for left-handers.

FORCED BACKWARDS I FIND IT LESS RESTRICTING TO LEAD WITH THE 'WRONG' FOOT

LESSON 28
SKID BOAST UNDER PRESSURE

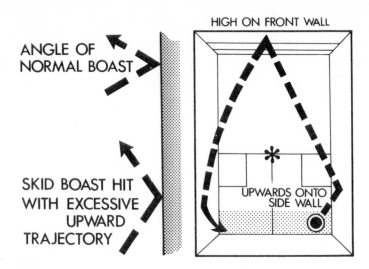

ANGLE OF NORMAL BOAST

SKID BOAST HIT WITH EXCESSIVE UPWARD TRAJECTORY

HIGH ON FRONT WALL

UPWARDS ONTO SIDE WALL

When one is under pressure in the back of the court there is little point in playing a hard-hit boast just above the tin. An error is likely: It's do or die—and the opponent will probably be balanced near the T ready to move smoothly to pick up and punish anything other than a dead-nick.

A shot that provides at least some solution is a high boast. Now commonly called the skid-boast this shot can be devastatingly effective. It is most disconcerting when you have buried your opponent in the back of the court, to find that he has hit the ball almost like a drive down the wall (see diagram), but so that it catches the side wall in front of him with a sweeping upward trajectory and comes high off the front wall and spirals back over your head.

Nasrullah's brother, Roshan Khan, who was once world champion first displayed this stroke, and his technique in this regard has been copied by many of the young Pakistanis to good effect.

LESSON 29
CLASSIC LET

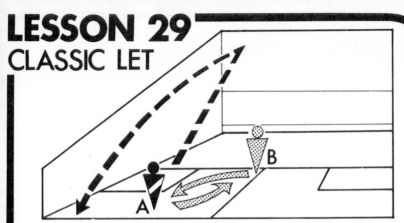

IN THIS SITUATION 'A' HAS PLAYED A GOOD
LENGTH. 'A' MAKES FOR THE 'T'-'B' MAKES FOR
THE BALL RESULTING IN A COLLISION. THE RULES
STATE THAT 'A' MUST GET OUT OF 'B's' WAY –
IN FACT IF B WAS UNLIKELY TO PLAY A WINNER
FROM THIS STROKE THEN A LET IS ALLOWED.

An interpretation of the rules could fill a manual in itself.
Perhaps I might supply just a little general guidance here.
Where a player is intentionally, even wilfully, obstructed,
whether he may or may not have struck a winner, he will
be given the point. Should the obstruction be accidental,
but nevertheless prevent an almost certain winner, there
again a penalty point must be awarded.

If the obstruction is accidental, which I hasten to add is
the rule rather than the exception, but a return would have
been made, then an automatic let is given—that is really
the classic let. The drawing shows an accidental
obstruction by player 'A'; player 'B' could have returned
the ball, but was unlikely to have hit a winner, so the
point is played again.

Provided 'A' is making the effort to clear, the let should
be automatic. Strictly, 'A' should completely clear the path,
but 'B' might perhaps have moved a little early and it then
becomes more difficult for 'A' to clear.

Referees will always be criticised. Top players much
prefer their matches to be controlled by one another.
If a referee remains consistent in his decisions, whether
the players agree with his interpretation or not, they will
accept him in his own right.

LESSON 30
CLASSIC PENALTY POINT

PLAYER A
CROSSES THE
PATH OF THE BALL
IN TRYING TO REACH
THE T - RESTRICTING
HIS OPPONENT'S
RETURN & RISKING
INJURY

Perhaps an even greater area of friction between players surrounds the use of the penalty point—the awarding of a point to one player who has been placed either accidentally or otherwise at an unfair disadvantage by a stroke, movement, or tactic of the other. All of us have an opponent who always seems to be in our way but it is even less satisfactory if he rarely pays for it.

When you have completed your stroke you must allow your opponent to move directly to the ball. Any lethargy in this area can result in a penalty point. Perhaps the classic penalty point, illustrated here, is where player 'A' has tried to strike a ball down the side wall but finds that the ball has flown inaccurately and is coming back at him or even on the other side (follow in the drawing).

In his attempt to retrieve the central position at the T, he jumps across the line of the ball thereby placing himself in grave danger of being struck by his opponent's racket, or by the ball, as the opponent tries to move in to take it early.

Too frequently the offender gets away with it because his opponent is either gentle or believes in mercy, or both, and merely lets the ball go to the back wall. But our gentleman is now placed at a disadvantage at the back and, if I were refereeing, I would stop play and award him a well-justified classic penalty point.

If a player stops his stroke when he could have hit his opponent, there must be a penalty awarded. However, I don't feel that one can judge that a certain winner would have been made from the back of the court and under almost all other circumstances in that area, I would award a let ball.

LESSON 31
TURNING OUT OF CORNERS

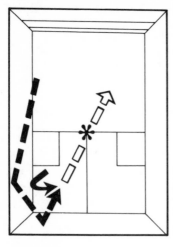

TO COUNTER AN OVERHIT
LENGTH A PLAYER MAY
SWIVEL AROUND TO
REACH THE BALL

Turning is within the rules, but also dangerous and has too frequently been used as a weapon of intimidation. The argument that if your opponent turns it is because you have played a bad length ball—overhit in fact—is not wholly acceptable. Quite frequently the only recourse left to a player when he has been harried unmercifully into one of the back corners by a really good length ball is to attempt to play out on the turn. Sometimes the opponent does turn because of an overhit ball—your fault; sometimes because of accurate length—your good play.

In either instance you should not have to take evasive action which almost certainly means losing the point, and suffering being struck by the ball—at best uncomfortable. It is possible to contest arguments for and against turning, good length and bad length. I think the most important factor is the amount of danger involved to the average player. The top competitor has a good reflex system—like a matador—but not all players can expect to measure distance and react in the same way. One rule for the minority and another for the majority would be far too complicated.

I feel that the two arguments are valid but the safety factor is too vital to ignore. I would ban altogether the turning movement from the game.

LESSON 32
DANGEROUS PLAY

It is very easy to be dangerous on a Squash court. I have been cut badly round the left eye on approximately seventeen occasions in eight years of play. That my eye has withstood this rather savage onslaught so nobly is a tribute to my Maker. That I have been brutally molested so frequently could be for a number of reasons. My opponents dislike me intensely—highly probable; I am loath to remove myself from the path of an eager enemy—certainly true as my energy evaporates; that he fails to control his follow-through when attempting to belt the ball—Ah!—the truth is out at last.

The game of Squash at a high level is ruthless in its demands on mental and physical efficiency. However, players are generally fair and hardly ever guilty of wilful assault and battery. The most dangerous aspect of our game—the over-wielding of the racket on backswing and follow-through occurs only rarely. At a lower level the overswing is almost certainly accidental and due to the lack of fundamental coaching. Players don't at first know how to strike the ball safely.

Squash should remain an exhibition of racket skill and physical athleticism. The top competitive Squash players soon ensure that anyone too prone to unreasonable behaviour is given some corrective instruction. Let any guilty player within your club or circle realise that he will shortly run out of opponents if he doesn't mend his ways. Perhaps this book will at least teach the growing squash population just a little about the art of survival.

HUMILITY? NO!
EVADING
UNREASONABLE
BEHAVIOUR

DIET AND SQUASH

Almost daily I am asked about my own diet. I think many people imagine I spend most of my life in the trees eating bananas, nuts and raisins. I have been called many uncomplimentary things but sometimes I do indeed feel more kinship with animals and primitives. Yet I had a perfectly normal, civilised British up-bringing and ate the usual foods, although many things were rationed and they didn't let me have my orange juice after the age of six—curse them!

Lack of discipline is at the heart of our inadequacy and is the common enemy of us all. Moderation in everything but hard work seems to be the preaching of the Puritans, but temperance in eating and drinking provides for better general health—what greater incentive?—and leads to greater satisfaction when participating on the Squash-court—the pleasure of doing something better and even winning sometimes!!

Because I am generally involved in training and practice routines throughout each day, I find it easier to exist on

24 HOURS
ALCOHOL
CHINESE FOOD
CURRIES ETC.

7 HOURS
MEAT   ONIONS
MUSHROOMS
TOMATOES
FRESH FRUIT

well sugared tea and the odd honey sandwich. However, by eventide the schedule is completed and then I can be reasonably compared to a vacuum cleaner. Substantial amounts of meat and fish—my protein content—and vast amounts of potatoes and other starch foods disappear effortlessly. The *pièce de résistance* remains—the pudding course is where I lose all discipline and overindulge my eternal fancy for ice-cream, chocolate cake, trifles and anything rich and sweet—superb carbohydrate content which filters over a period of time into my system and regenerates me for the morrow and thereafter. Whilst most necessary for me, this sort of diet will in time kill off most others. My day is intensely active and I am constantly burning up the calories. For any man or woman in a sedentary occupation there has to be a much smaller intake of those starches and lovely sweet destroyers.

There are few things worse than playing an arduous sport on a full stomach. The digestive system is never placed under greater strain and too many sportsmen, both amateur and professional, still insist on a good steak three hours or less before commencing battle. One day common-sense may prevail and players will appreciate the necessity of a sensible diet prior to competition.

4 HOURS
MILK FISH CHEESE
OMELETTES

3 HOURS
EGG TOAST
CRISPS ICE CREAM
BREAD AND JAM

1 HOUR
TEA WITH SUGAR

We all vary considerably in our powers of digestion but there is only real value from food taken in many hours before participation in the game. Certainly the protein benefit comes from the meals on the day before and it is as well to ensure that all spicy foods such as curries are last eaten twenty-four hours or so before the start.

It is also sensible to take your last drop of alcohol twenty-four hours before competition. I rarely drink alcohol because I spent too many of my formative years trying to impair my modest faculties by drowning them daily in liquor. However, a little never did anyone any harm.

I think that most players prefer to eat a meal of some substance before they play. I feel a good lunch six to seven hours before an evening match is quite sensible and that foods such as meat, salads, mushrooms and fresh fruit can all be eaten. Nasrullah gave me this habit at the beginning of our coach/pupil relationship. I have retained it when possible ever since. He would allow me the odd cup of well-sugared tea during the often extremely tense interim period. He always said: 'Never get nervous on a full stomach or you might see your food again !'

Sometimes four hours before the contest, if I haven't had an opportunity earlier, I will have a light omelette, even a little fish and a glass of milk. But even if time is starting to run out and I still haven't eaten I will never take in anything of substance later than three hours before going on court. If I do so I can't benefit and one day might suffer permanent harm. A poached egg, or cheese on toast, a few chips, ice-cream, even better bread and jam or honey—all these I have found a comfort, if nothing else ! The traditional cup of sweet tea an hour before the curtain goes up rounds off my dietary preparation nicely.

In general terms I drink plenty of liquid, mostly water, use a frightening amount of salt in humid climates and never smoke. Had I smoked there would not have been a manual—moderation in that habit is still just not good enough.

BARRINGTON THINKING

I should imagine my own thinking on court is quite similar to many other top players, although we vary considerably in the application thereof. Players at all levels should have some kind of pattern, if only to make a tricky game a little less complicated.

Everything seems to happen so quickly in Squash that even the minutest amount of method can alleviate the madness of conflict! While a great part of my thinking cannot be applied in practice to its ultimate conclusion without an especial form of training far beyond the time quota of the average player, he can at least find in my own thinking a guideline to the format of his game and even choose one point relative to himself, perhaps a weakness, which he can now try to erase.

Self-examination is more difficult for the leading Squash players than for those in other sports because they so rarely see themselves depicted on film. But a continual self-analysis is advisable and in this way one can become much more capable of learning from victory as well as defeat.

I am only interested in one objective—winning. That is my all-consuming motivation, and the most powerful stimulus. Regardless of any friendship outside, on the court the opponent is a deadly enemy and I intend to destroy him—to do so is to survive.

Before I even reach the court I am well aware of the game I shall try to impose on *most* of my opponents. This I can adapt in play should the situation so demand, or prior to the battle should I be faced with an unusual opponent. I *know* in the changing room that I will knock-up, or hit-up, while preparing myself for the wholesale destruction about to take place! I will not puncture the tin in the preparation period, nor hit with full power until well warmed up. A sensible, accurate series of placements, mainly back to the opponent, is the best foundation. I shall gauge the pace of the court, check out the brightness, or lack of, in the lighting, and systematically bring myself to the 'moment of truth'.

When war is finally declared, whether serving or not, I shortly let the enemy know that the initial engagement will be brutally fought and no quarter given. Where armies are well-matched, any military historian worth his salt will tell us that neither initially will run amok, but with tremendous determination will sound each other out playing the percentages, eschewing the gamble, until a chink is exposed and the pressure is then further imposed.

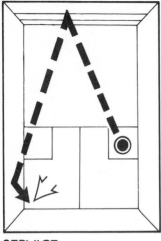

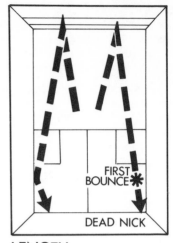

FIRST BOUNCE ✳

DEAD NICK

SERVICE   LENGTH

My strategy is such and I am conveniently more certain of a breakthrough because I know that he knows that I am the fitter man.

The basis of my game is *length*. Rallies are so much easier to win when the opposition has been confined to the rear by length strokes—Naz always insists that when the enemy had been so placed there comes a time when he is 'out of sight, out of mind', and the front-court balls can be happily played. When I am out-of-hand (the receiver), I am committed to getting the service back, by very exact percentage play, never granting a free point with an unforced error. My opponent is going to be made to realise that he has to *win* the point. I frustrate him with relentless length play and only place the ball short when I have almost carried him through the door or into the gallery! I only hit short from behind when extricating myself from a back corner and then that short ball will bounce high on the front wall enabling me to recover my position.

Now I have won the service and the thinking changes. I am still applying my fundamental length method, but there will be continual harassment and a much more positive attack. If I make an error the enemy gets the service and not a point—so all is not lost. Killing strokes are still played on the percentage basis—preferably when in front of the opponent and well-balanced, using drops and nick-kills.

I can now make more use of the strokes from behind

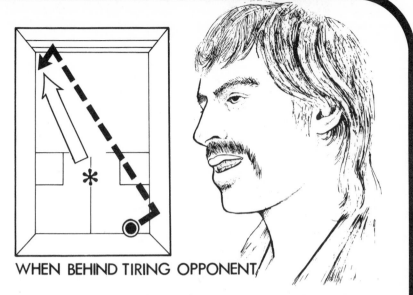

WHEN BEHIND TIRING OPPONENT

my opponent and I find the boast is increasingly effective as he tires (see drawing). All variations can be used but remember the best results come with discretion. Remember too that when you come to serve, you have a simple superiority—you have the ball and he has to wait for the 'Molotov Cocktail' to arrive. Ensure that it is explosive!

A final thought. I have so often been called ultra-defensive, just a physical machine devoid of strokes. There are so many 'pretty losers' and anybody can try for the dazzling winner and on occasions receive rapturous applause, and LOSE. Those players never win big matches but their reputations are sadly glamourised by the so-called cognoscenti. The hardest strokes to play and the best are the 'clingers', where the ball is brought so close to the side walls. Points are won outright or lead to winners, because the opponent can't return or does so badly. These 'lucky, boring,' frustrating strokes are a central thread in my thinking. The gallery remains mute as the enraged enemy is drawn insidiously into the spider's web. Even Taleb, that magnificent Merlin of strokeplay, at his best would set up his opponents with simple, basic Squash before reducing them to frustration, and finally exhaustion, with his stupendous array of well-practised killing strokes. But now, dogged in play by fear of his own lack of fitness, he has become a 'pretty loser'.

The Khans have taught me the language of the game. No pupil could have wished for better masters.

LESSON 33
TRAINING OFF COURT

'You must devil up your muscles'—so spoke the oracle, my coach Nasrullah Khan in 1966. He prescribed a general course of weight-training at least three times a week under Reub Martin at the Mayfair Gymnasium in

London to build-up a body hitherto an advertisement for emaciation. Weights under supervision remain a very important part of my training. I know what the Mayfair Gymnasium has done for me and I am infuriated when I hear the ignorant pontificating on the ill-effects of weight-training—slows you down, distorts your body, makes you muscle-bound.

What a load of cobblers! Just ask my opponents. Any ambitious young player will benefit from a general course in weights—whether he's doing composite exercises on an interval basis, a form of circuit training, or steady work with somewhat heavier weights. Supervision is most important to learn correct posture and technique—thanks to Reub and Wally Schulberg, his partner, I rapidly developed a blend of strength and speed. Man, with the advance of science, has been reduced to a state of apathy and obesity.

'Man was a hunter, so are you; he ran, you will run—this is very good thing'—Naz Khan 1966. So I ran, with no system, no pattern, but proving to myself as the months went by, that running is the foundation of physical fitness, and a necessary side to training for any stress sport where the legs, heart and lungs are worked to exhaustion point. It was Derek Ibbotson, the great athlete, who taught me how to train properly in the open. This involves using steady mileage as a background, varying this with faster work, free-running, and then building in more and more speed work—anything from 50 yds to 440 yds on an interval basis with timed recovery. I try to plan my competitive year so that from February through to July I can concentrate on a background build-up which will have adequately prepared me for, and will sustain me through, a long tour over five or six months when I will be playing every day. During this time I ease my running schedule but will maintain a constant daily repetition of press-ups and abdominal exercises and any other perverse forms of torture I may devise.

Sometimes I feel I have had enough of living in that sterile little cell, the Squash court, and I involve myself even more intensively in the other training variations. That brings me safely through what people call 'a stale patch' and it is much more valuable than a complete rest, after which the muscles have to learn to adapt again to the movement of our extraordinary sport.

LESSON 34
TRAINING ON COURT

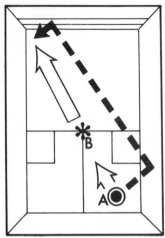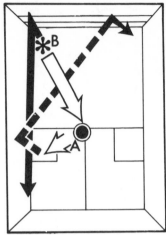

'A' STARTS WITH A BOAST TO THE FRONT –
'B' MOVES TO THE BALL, PLAYS A STRAIGHT
DRIVE & RETURNS TO THE T POSITION.
'A' INTERCEPTS & BOASTS; 'B' GOES FORWARD ETC

Court-training and practice with a partner can be most rewarding. Where one player may be of a much higher standard than the other, and any game between them would be a pointless 'no contest', each can help himself and the other by practising certain routines together.

The first exercise can be used by players of almost any standard and this one is illustrated well in the diagram. Quite simply, the player in front has to concentrate on straight drives to the back of the court and the man behind plays continual boasts. So player A hits the ball down the right forehand wall and B plays a boast which takes the ball and player A up to the top left-hand corner, from where he plays his straight backhand drive. B moves across to boast on his backhand side and so the routine is repeated until a mistake is induced or a winner is made.

A concentrates on a gobbling stride to the ball, orthodox positioning of feet, a drive which pushes B well to the rear, and then with his racket head up, *long movement back to the T*. The last is most important and must be part of the routine. B moves swiftly to left and right, always returning, albeit briefly, near to the T position—and remembers the 'wrong foot' movement, particularly when getting the ball out of the forehand back corner.

This exercise will undoubtedly improve at least three vital facets of your game—firstly, *ball control*; constant repetition of either a drive or a boast must improve these strokes; secondly, *movement*; working from the T to the front and back again or to the side or rear and back, under constant pressure, must improve a player's footwork; thirdly, *physical fitness*; this is a killing process when due attention is taken to returning to the T position after striking the ball.

The routine can be taken further by permitting the leading player to hit the ball across the court as well as straight and the player behind can add the straight and cross-court drops to his repertoire.

The second routine should be tried by players eager to reach the top. It develops the necessary reflex qualities and a confidence on the volley. Player B takes the T position and now has to rule the kingdom along the short line at half-court. No ball, hard or soft, from player A working behind him, must pass his racket.

His objective is to volley or drive, if A feeds them short, all balls to the back corners of the court. He must remember to bring the racket head up after completion of the stroke and to follow the course of the ball behind him, otherwise he has no chance. This is a most demanding exercise for the leading player and when the going becomes just too tough, the players reverse roles.

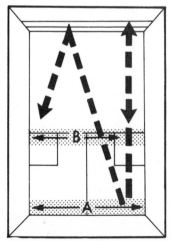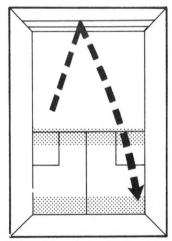

A DRIVES THE BALL HIGH OR LOW, STRAIGHT OR ACROSS COURT – B INTERCEPTS THE BALL AND HITS DEEP (REPEAT ROUTINE)

MENTAL DOMINATION

✱ HASHIM KHAN   **◉ MAHMOUD KARIM**

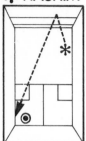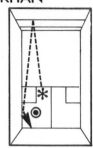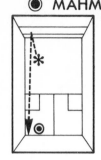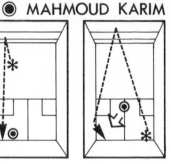

'The mind in battle' is an absorbing study, and the mental aspect of the game should be a vital link in the player's preparation.

Before playing my major matches I would be geared by Nasrullah to expect great things of myself. Naz had built his pupil on firm ground and whatever might happen on the day, he knew I would utilise my growing strength. The harsh training gave me supreme confidence and my opponents were made well aware of that. I have been taught to stress them mentally even before I may get to them physically ; to impose protracted rallies on them from the outset, so that the message of pain will be intolerably clear, a massive payment of mind and body demanded of them before victory might be attained.

Conversely, a vital link in the domination chain takes place when I am under severe pressure. It is then that I must be icily resolute, emotionally unhindered by the mental discomfort of a difficult position. Under these circumstances I *must* continue to call on my basic training, a precision performance of mind and body, retaining discipline with percentage play and the odd luxury of a calculated gamble. This link is perhaps the most priceless part of mental domination. It is relatively simple to remain coldly self-contained when the wind is favourable, but hardly so when faced by a howling gale.

In his First British Open Final with Karim in 1950 Hashim Khan provided a classic example of mental domination. With an absorbing match nicely balanced at 5–5 in the first, throughout one monumental rally, the ambitious Pakistani plotted *every* return deep to the Egyptian's backhand (see drawing). Karim had never before faced such an 'unsporting' (!) assault, finally lost the point, cracked mentally, and failed to score again. Hashim really was the greatest !

BARRINGTON'S BRUTAL BATTLES 6

FINAL VICTORY

BRITISH OPEN CHAMPIONSHIP						FINAL
FEBRUARY 5 1972 SHEFFIELD	GAME 1	2	3	4	5	POINTS
JONAH BARRINGTON IRELAND	0	9	10	5	9	
GEOFF HUNT AUSTRALIA	9	7	8	9	7	

A full year without any competition and beset by a series of illnesses had left me very unsure of what I could produce in my first confrontation with Geoff Hunt in eighteen months. That he was playing really well as a professional was more obvious and when his confident game was weighed against my own inevitable lack of practice and assurance, he appeared as a firm favourite with the pundits. The field had been terribly strong throughout the championship, and the atmosphere electric as the players battled their way towards the final on the new and magnificent exhibition court at the Abbeydale Club.

In an interview Hunt had firmly stated he was going for a reasonably quick, positive win. He had worked hard on his attack while touring with Ken Hiscoe and now was aggressively grooved. I intimated that as far as I was concerned, the battle had to be extremely long for me to win, and I intended to win. I hoped Hunt would force from the beginning and make a few errors before getting into a rhythm. He had done this before, presenting me with the first game and thereby committing himself to at least another three. It had cost him dear in the past.

This time it was not to be—he had learned his lesson, unhappily for me, too well. From the start the man was like a machine, fast onto the ball, clipping it ruthlessly to the back corners and then utilising the boast to move me to the front. I could not stretch the initial engagement beyond fifteen minutes, and I still had not scored by the end of it. In fact I was becoming almost unfamiliar with the service by that time! The Australian had me constantly floundering and harried me into errors—the pressure was so much more intense than anything I had met in a long time. He seemed to read my strokes before I had even considered them and he certainly showed no sign of stress when I managed to work him a little.

A quick chat with Nasrullah between games decided my tactics from then on. I could not afford to put Geoff short unless he was almost sitting in the gallery and the only time he was contained was when the ball was high on his backhand side. I now waged a total war of attrition. He continued to score but the rallies were lengthening and he didn't like them. At 0–4 in the second I at last got to him.

The service changed hands five times with neither of us gaining ground and then finally I squeezed an error out of him. My first point had arrived after twenty-seven minutes. Now the battle was really joined and the gap narrowed as Geoff hit his first tiredness barrier. Helped by a penalty point I moved to game ball and then staved off the Hunt assault. From 5–8 he came to 7–8—the vital point eluded him even though he saved five game points. Finally I was on level terms when he failed to get hold of a good service. The game had lasted nearly thirty minutes and I had started to draw his sting.

But Geoff can be excessively weary one minute and then like the superb athlete he is, almost fully recovered in the next. The interval gave him fresh strength and in a dazzling burst of attack he flew to 6–1 in the third. But the effort had depleted him again, the ball kept on coming back, and he lapsed into mistakes. I drew level at 6–6 and there was a long breathtaking rally during which we explored every tactic to gain the ascendancy—it ended on a let, but it had left its mark on both of us.

I was the first to weaken and Hunt went on to 8–6 on a penalty point. The situation was now critical, and I took the offensive and came out fighting. 7–8 and back on terms with a penalty point. It was clearly an incorrect decision. But the game must throw in injustices. These are rarely malicious and must be bravely borne. Geoff lost his temper, quickly hit the tin twice, presented the game on a plate and must still be kicking himself. I had taken the lead and I knew he had never beaten me in five in competition.

Depressed he may have been, but his temperament was back in order at the beginning of the fourth. I led 1–0 but then felt quite ill for some ten minutes. Sensing this he put in another powerful burst and my trusty lob for the first time failed me. Although he came back to me towards the end of the fourth he was never in any real danger of losing it and must have felt pretty elated at the sudden change in his fortune.

The fifth seemed to support this conclusion as Geoff again showed all his early bounce and remorselessly headed for home. At 0–6, out of hand, I collected my wits and played my last cards—a series of much faster rallies which took him by surprise. At 2–6 he was almost gone again and the weariness had turned him chalky white. Yet I made an error and he advanced to within two points of the championship with a clear cut penalty point. Dicky Rutnagur of *The Daily Telegraph*, wrote:

'Geoff was only two points from victory, but the nearness of it was not a potent enough tonic to revive him for the final effort. The numbness of fatigue set in and the racket head began to droop as he addressed the ball. In breathless silence Jonah went from 4–7 to 7 all. Geoff could not now get in front and Jonah finished off the match with two winning volleys.'

It had been yet another shattering experience but the satisfaction of success was a fulfilling reward for the mental and physical discomfort suffered throughout that year and those long gone by, and it was yet another springboard towards so many pain-barriers in the future.

LESSON 35
INDIVIDUAL TRAINING ON COURT

'GHOSTING'
TIMED STRESS SESSIONS
ONE MINUTE ON STRIKING
AN IMAGINARY BALL FOLLOWED
BY ONE MINUTE RECOVERY

The peerless Hashim Khan describes in his book how he used to chase the ball round the court on his own—Hashim v Hashim! Naz gave me this system to develop my own stamina for the game. As I work from corner to corner using drives, boasts, drops and lobs, there is no pleasure in the thrill of the chase, merely a very painful oxygen debt—again can't breathe—and lactic acid build-up in the legs—can't walk, let alone run! This simple form of torture, when applied consistently for a specific period of time with short recoveries will inevitably give you a greater degree of fitness.

A method developed by myself over the last two years has also proved to be most valuable. This is called 'ghosting', so named because it is done without the ball and not because of any ghosts involved—no self-respecting spectre could possibly allow himself to be heard to breathe so heavily.

The object of 'ghosting' is to simulate the playing of the game as closely as possible but in so doing one is in fact putting the body under much greater stress, more frequently, than would happen in a game. At the same time discipline in movement and in striking the imaginary ball is of paramount importance. Constant movement from the T to any part of the court and the recovery to the central position is meticulously observed. The animal crouch, the long gobbling stride, striking through the ball, no short-cuts, a timed stress session of perhaps one minute intervals (one minute on and one minute recovery); try five and five recoveries—ten minutes. Work up to ten and a twenty minutes work-load. Play around with the recovery time—sometimes more, sometimes less.

When working to a peak I use up to forty minutes—twenty agonising pain barriers and twenty recoveries—hardly the word!

Count the movements from the T to a corner and back as one. Dart to the side, to play a volley or smash and back to the central position, a second movement. You should work for between twenty-two and thirty movements in one minute. That imaginary opponent would have given even Hashim a hard time. Try it, but see your medical adviser first.

LESSON 36
THINK AT ALL TIMES

There have been many great 'thinkers' off the court but too few in the actual game of 'physical chess'. When I first came onto the Squash scene, the British Professor was a left-hander called Richard Boddington. Deficient in the more spectacular killing strokes, he nevertheless cultivated the nasty habit of shattering his opponents with a remorseless pattern of sensible, logical play.

On the professional level, Azam Khan had been out of competition for a couple of years but I will never again encounter such a calculating Squash competitor. Apart from being a mind-reader—there should be a rule against that—he reduced the game to simplicities and quietly, almost apologetically, did a clinical dissection of those foolish enough to offer themselves before the altar and even sometimes to conspire his overthrow—dirty devils!

He was once playing a young British hope who gathered one solitary point only in three swift games. The aspirant was complaining about the number of times he had planted the ball into the tin and begged Azam to advise him on the matter. The reply was simple, as is his custom: 'Hit the ball little bit higher!'

I am at the end of my treatise and am beginning to wonder to what degree I may have undermined your game with my coaching and your health with the exercises. Squash is a game of habits, good or bad. These become ingrained in your system over a period of time and are used instinctively once the game begins and the fever of the fight takes its hold of you. I am going to leave you with one simple thought—the simple things being the most difficult to attain; whether you are practising on your own or with a partner, playing friendly games, or competitive games at club or international level, try not to allow your heart to rule your head; continue to calculate the percentage reward of each stroke in relation to the position of your imaginary or very real opponent, and

SIMPLY REMEMBER TO THINK AT ALL TIMES.

SQUASH FOR ALL

Once upon a time a few schoolboys waiting for their turn to play a game called racquets passed the time outside the court by hitting a soft ball against a wall. It turned out to be good fun and one or two decided to take if further. At the same time those in debt in the Fleet Prison—kindred spirits of mine—also whiled away the lonely hours in similar vein. From such strange beginnings has sprung a game which is rapidly finding its place as a necessary social habit and major modern leisure force in Britain and throughout the world.

At my worst moments I am quite convinced that Squash is an invention of the devil—in many matches I seem to go through a form of concentrated hell! But there are so many good days and moments of pure happiness which can only be attributed to the game I love to play and hate to lose!

At present our clubs multiply by the month and the oversubscribed courts are unable to cope. Where will the game go from here? I see it one day as a grand spectacle on television—so beware those who doubt! To surmount the visual disadvantages there will be courts with see-through walls and the faithful will flock to see their favourites, the heroes and the villains. The Japanese will make the greatest impact on the game, first of all in the commercial sense and then competitively. They will relish the disciplines and dedication, so necessary, and yet so appalling to most.

Yes, Squash Rackets has come a long way and is no longer in bondage. Once a game administered by the few for the few, its future lies with the many. One day there will be Squash for the housewife and Squash for the hippy; indeed it will become a game for all.